DIS

This book has been ___ ___ ___ intention of simplifying the complex concepts related to Generative AI and Artificial Intelligence for the reader's understanding. Every effort has been made to provide the most accurate and easy-to-understand explanations at the time of writing.

However, it is important to acknowledge that the field of AI is dynamic and rapidly evolving. Innovations and breakthroughs are occurring at an exponential rate, and information that is accurate today may be superseded by new findings or technologies tomorrow.

While I have done my utmost to ensure the content is clear, structured, and as current as possible, the fast-paced nature of this field might result in some information becoming outdated post-publication.

Please consider this book as a foundation and guide for your exploration of AI and Generative AI, but not as an exhaustive, up-to-the-minute source of information. Always supplement your learning with additional research, especially from trusted and current academic, scientific, and industry resources, to keep up-to-date with the most recent developments in this exciting field

COPYRIGHT

BASICS OF AI

Have you ever seen a sci-fi movie where robots can talk, think, and act like humans? Well, that's what we call Artificial Intelligence or AI. But don't worry, we're not in a movie, and AI is not just about talking robots. It's actually a very interesting and important part of our everyday life.

Let's make it simple. AI is like teaching a computer to act like a human. Just like when we teach a pet dog to fetch a ball. We throw the ball, and the dog runs and brings it back. After a few tries, the dog learns that bringing back the ball makes us happy, and we give it a treat. Similarly, we can teach computers to understand and learn from information or 'data', as we call it in the world of computers.

So, how do we do that? Well, we give the computer lots and lots of data. For example, if we want to teach a computer to recognize a cat, we would show it thousands of pictures of cats. After seeing so many cat pictures, the computer will start to notice things that all cats have in common - like pointy ears, whiskers, and a tail. This way, it can learn to recognize a cat.

This is just like how we learn. When we were babies, we didn't know what a cat was. But after seeing a few cats, we started to understand what a cat looks like. AI works the same way. It learns from data, just like we learn from our experiences.

You might not know it, but you use AI every day. Have you ever used Google to find information? Or asked Siri, Alexa, or Google Assistant a question? That's AI! These systems learn from the things you search or ask. The more you use them, the better they get at understanding what you want.

This is called 'training the model'. Just like we train our pet dog to fetch the ball, we train AI systems to understand and learn from data. Over time, they get better and better at making sense of the data.

But AI isn't perfect. Just like how our pet dog sometimes fetches the wrong ball, AI can also make mistakes. That's because AI is only as good as the data it learns from. If the data is incorrect or biased, AI can make wrong or unfair decisions.

That's why it's important for us to use AI responsibly. We should make sure that the data we use to train AI is accurate and fair. And we should always check the decisions made by AI to make sure they are correct and fair.

AI is a powerful tool. It can help us find information, answer questions, and even drive cars! But like any tool, it's important to use it wisely. So next time you use Google, Siri, Alexa, or Google Assistant, remember, you're using AI!

AI is not just about talking robots. It's about teaching

computers to understand and learn from data. It's a fun and exciting field that is changing our world every day.

What is Intelligence?

Intelligence is a fascinating and complex concept that humans have been trying to define and understand for centuries. It is an integral part of our everyday lives, influencing how we learn, how we solve problems, and how we interact with the world around us. At its core, intelligence is the capacity to acquire, understand, and apply knowledge. It involves the ability to reason, solve problems, think abstractly, comprehend complex ideas, learn quickly, and learn from experience.

To illustrate this, consider a common scenario. You're playing a new video game for the first time. In the beginning, you're unfamiliar with the controls, the game mechanics, and the objectives. However, as you continue to play, you begin to understand how the game works. You start recognizing patterns, making connections, and developing strategies. This is your intelligence at work.

Intelligence is not just about learning and understanding, it's also about adapting and applying what you've learned. Let's say you've been baking cakes using a specific recipe. One day, you run out of a particular ingredient. Instead of giving up, you remember reading about a possible substitute. You decide to use this substitute and, to your delight, the cake turns out great. This ability to adapt and apply knowledge is another facet of intelligence.

DEFINING ARTIFICIAL INTELLIGENCE

So, by now you know a little about AI, right? But what exactly does it mean? It's kind of like when we talk about a person being intelligent, but here, we're talking about machines. Essentially, it's when we try to make machines and computers behave a bit like humans, where they can understand, learn, and even make decisions based on what they've learned.

Let's say you're playing chess with a computer. You make a move, and then the computer makes a move. But how does it decide what move to make? Well, that's where AI comes in. It looks at the current state of the game, thinks about all the possible moves it could make, and then decides on the best one. And here's the cool part - it learns from each game it plays, so it keeps getting better and better over time!

Now, when we talk about AI, there are a couple of terms you might hear quite often - Machine Learning and Deep Learning. They're like the building blocks of AI.

Machine Learning is a way for computers to learn from data. Here , the chess playing computer uses machine learning to understand the patterns in the game and improve its strategy. It's a bit like when you study for a test. You read through the material, try to understand the patterns and connections, and then use that knowledge to answer the questions in the exam.

Deep Learning, on the other hand, is a bit more complex. It's a subset of machine learning that tries to mimic the way our brains work. You see, our brains are made up of billions of tiny units called neurons, and they're all interconnected in a vast network. In deep learning, we create artificial neural networks that try to replicate this structure. These networks can learn from vast amounts of data and can even recognize complex patterns that would be difficult for a human to spot.

Another important aspect of AI is Natural Language Processing (NLP). This is the technology that allows computers to understand and generate human language. Think of your interactions with Siri or Alexa. You ask a question, and they respond almost as if they understood what you said. That's NLP at work!

AI has the potential to transform our world in ways we can't even imagine yet. From self-driving cars to personalized education, from predicting natural disasters to making healthcare more efficient - the possibilities are endless. But like any powerful tool, it comes with its own set of challenges and ethical considerations. As we continue to develop and integrate AI into our lives, it's important for us to consider how it's used and ensure that it benefits everyone.

Understanding Artificial Intelligence:

Narrow AI and General AI

Artificial Intelligence (AI) has become a pivotal part of our daily lives, subtly influencing various aspects from the way we shop to how we work and communicate. To fully comprehend the essence of AI, it's crucial to understand its two main types: Narrow AI and General AI. In this discussion, we'll delve deeper into what these two types entail, their current applications, their future potential, and the challenges associated with them.

Narrow AI: The Specialist

Narrow AI, also known as Weak AI, is a type of AI that is designed to perform a single task. It's like a highly skilled artist who is a master at painting but doesn't know how to do anything else. A perfect example is a spam filter for your email. This AI is excellent at identifying and filtering out unwanted emails but can't perform tasks outside of that.

Other examples of Narrow AI include recommendation systems like those used by Netflix or Amazon to suggest movies or products based on your previous activity. Siri, Alexa, and other virtual assistants are also examples of Narrow AI, performing tasks like setting alarms, making phone calls, or playing music.

Despite being termed "weak," Narrow AI is highly effective within its designed task. Its strength lies in its ability to learn and improve at that specific task, making it more efficient over time.

General AI: The Multitalented Superstar

General AI, also known as Strong AI or Artificial General Intelligence (AGI), is the type of AI that can understand, learn, and apply knowledge across a wide range of tasks. It's similar to a multitalented individual who can paint, play the piano, write novels, and more.

General AI mimics human intelligence in its flexibility. It means that the AI can understand, learn, and then use that knowledge to solve problems, regardless of the domain. This is a concept that's not yet fully realized. Current AI technologies are still far from achieving this level of autonomy and versatility. General AI is more a goal for the future than a reality.

The Future Potential and Challenges

The future potential of both Narrow and General AI is immense. Narrow AI will continue to get better at specific tasks, making our lives more convenient. For instance, healthcare could benefit from Narrow AI that can analyze medical images with high accuracy, helping doctors in their diagnosis.

The concept of General AI, although not yet realized, holds transformative potential. A truly general AI could perform any intellectual task that a human being can, leading to significant breakthroughs in science, medicine, and many other fields.

However, the path to General AI is fraught with challenges. One of the main hurdles is our limited understanding of human intelligence itself. We're still in the process of understanding how human cognition works, and creating a machine that can mimic this is a monumental task.

Moreover, ethical considerations come into play with the development of General AI. How do we ensure that a highly intelligent machine acts in the best interest of humanity? How do we prevent misuse? These are questions that researchers are grappling with.

Both Narrow AI and General AI have their roles to play

in our future. While we're already reaping the benefits of Narrow AI, General AI remains largely a goal for the future. However, with rapid advancements in Artificial Intelligence (AI) is an area of computer science that focuses on creating machines and software that can mimic human intelligence. This fascinating field has been the subject of study and research for decades, and it's responsible for many of the technological advancements we enjoy today. From the voice assistant on your phone to the recommendation system on your favorite streaming service, AI is everywhere. But not all AI is created equal. It can be broadly categorized into two types: Narrow AI and General AI.

Narrow AI

Let's dive a bit more into Narrow AI. Imagine a world-class pianist who can flawlessly perform the most complicated pieces of music but struggles to paint a simple picture or cook a basic meal. The pianist is incredibly skilled in one specific area but lacks versatility. This is what Narrow AI is like. It's a type of AI that's designed to perform a single task extremely well.

Narrow AI is the most common form of AI that we encounter in our daily lives. It's the technology behind email spam filters, voice recognition systems, and online customer support bots. These AI systems are excellent at what they do, but they're limited to their specific tasks. The spam filter, for example, is great at identifying and blocking unwanted emails, but it can't help you write a business proposal or plan a dinner menu.

But don't let the term "narrow" fool you. Narrow AI can be incredibly complex and powerful. It's the driving force behind many cutting-edge technologies, including autonomous vehicles and sophisticated diagnostic tools in healthcare. However, despite its capabilities, Narrow AI lacks the ability to perform tasks beyond its programming. It's like a very talented artist who only knows how to paint but can't play a musical instrument or write a novel.

General AI

Now let's move on to General AI. Picture a multitalented superstar who can paint masterpieces, play several musical instruments, write bestselling novels, and even cook gourmet meals. This individual is proficient in many areas, demonstrating a versatility that's quite remarkable. This is what General AI aspires to be: a type of AI that can understand, learn, and apply knowledge across a wide range of tasks.

Unlike Narrow AI, General AI is not limited to a single task or domain. It's designed to mimic human intelligence, meaning it should be able to perform any intellectual task that a human being can do. It can learn from experience, understand complex concepts, solve problems, and even exhibit creativity.

However, as we discussed previously, General AI remains largely theoretical. While it's a fascinating concept that has been a subject of many science fiction stories, it's still not a reality. Creating an AI system that can truly understand, learn, and adapt like a human is a monumental challenge that scientists and researchers are still trying to overcome.

The Road Ahead

The journey from Narrow AI to General AI is not a simple one. It involves not just advancements in technology, but also addressing ethical considerations. How do we ensure that General AI is used for the betterment of society and not for destructive purposes? How do we deal with the potential impacts on the job market? These are complex questions that need to be answered as we move towards the future of AI.

In the meantime, Narrow AI continues to advance and impact various sectors. From healthcare and finance to transportation and entertainment, AI is revolutionizing how we live and work. It's helping doctors diagnose diseases, enabling cars to drive themselves, and personalizing our movie recommendations.

Despite the challenges, the future of AI looks promising. With continued research and innovation, the dream of creating a General AI might one day become a reality. But until then, we'll continue to benefit from the remarkable capabilities of Narrow AI.

In conclusion, while Narrow AI and General AI represent two ends of the AI spectrum

What is Machine Learning (ML)?

Machine Learning is a subset of AI. It's a method of data analysis that automates the building of analytical models. It allows computers to learn from data, identify patterns, and make decisions with minimal human intervention.

In traditional programming, developers write code to produce a certain output. In contrast, with machine learning, the machine is given a bunch of data and it learns to make predictions or decisions without being explicitly programmed to perform the task.

For example, a machine learning model can be trained to recognize cats by being shown thousands of pictures of cats. The model would identify patterns and features, like whiskers or tails, and use this information to recognize cats in the future.

What is Deep Learning (DL)?

Deep Learning is a subset of Machine Learning, which in turn is a subset of AI. It's inspired by the structure and function of the human brain, specifically the interconnections between neurons. Deep Learning models are built using artificial neural networks that mimic the neural connections in our brains.

The "deep" in Deep Learning refers to the depth of the neural network. A deep neural network has many layers of nodes between the input layer and the output layer. The more layers, the more complex patterns the network can recognize.

For example, in image recognition, initial layers might recognize simple patterns like lines and curves. Middle layers might recognize more complex features like shapes or eyes. The final layers might recognize high-level features like faces.

Deep Learning models are especially good at processing unstructured data, such as images, audio, or text. They excel in tasks like speech recognition, image recognition, and natural language processing.

Relationship between AI, ML, and DL

To understand the relationship between AI, ML, and DL, imagine three concentric circles. The largest circle represents AI, which is the broadest concept. The next smaller circle within AI is ML, and the smallest circle within ML is DL.

In other words, all Machine Learning is a type of Artificial Intelligence, and all Deep Learning is a type of Machine Learning.

To sum up, AI is the overarching concept of machines simulating human intelligence. Machine Learning is a technique to achieve AI where the machine learns from data without explicit programming. Deep Learning is a type of Machine Learning that uses artificial neural networks to model and understand complex patterns.

AI is making machines intelligent, ML is one way of doing it, and DL is a specific, powerful method of implementing ML.

Artificial Intelligence, or AI for short, is a fascinating field that's transforming the world as we know it. It's changing the way we work, play, and interact with technology. As we dive deeper into this intriguing topic, we'll discuss the two main types of AI: Narrow AI and General AI. We'll explore what they are, how they differ, and what their applications and challenges are.

to sum up:

- AI is the broadest concept, encompassing everything that involves machines simulating human intelligence.

- Machine Learning is a subset of AI that focuses on the ability of machines to receive a set of data and learn for themselves, changing algorithms as they learn more about the information they are processing.

- Deep Learning is a subset of Machine Learning that uses the concept of neural networks to solve complex problems, with the ability to learn, in a very real sense, from experience.

Introduction to Algorithms and How AI Learns

Imagine you're making a sandwich. You know you need to first take out two pieces of bread, apply some butter, put in your favorite filling, maybe add a slice of cheese, and finally put the other slice of bread on top. This step-by-step process is similar to what we call an algorithm in the world of AI.

An algorithm is simply a set of instructions that tells a computer what to do. Just like our sandwich recipe, an algorithm guides the computer through a process step-by-step to accomplish a specific goal, whether it's recognizing a face in a photo or translating a sentence from English to French.

AI, or Artificial Intelligence, refers to a broad field of study in computer science that aims to create systems that can perform tasks that normally require human intelligence. This includes things like understanding human speech, recognizing patterns, learning from experience, and making decisions. But how does AI learn to do these things?

The magic ingredient here is data. Data is like the fuel that powers the AI engine. You can think of data as a lot of examples that the AI can learn from. For instance, if we want to train an AI to recognize pictures of cats, we would show it thousands of pictures of cats. Each picture is a piece of data. The AI would analyze these pictures, look for patterns and common features, and learn what makes a cat a cat. This process is known as machine learning, which is a subset of AI.

Machine learning algorithms are designed to learn from data and make predictions or decisions without being explicitly programmed to do so. They use statistical techniques to learn patterns in the data. There are different types of machine learning algorithms, including supervised learning, where the algorithm learns from labeled data, and unsupervised learning, where the algorithm learns from unlabeled data by finding patterns and relationships within the data.

Neural networks, inspired by the human brain, are a type of machine learning algorithm that's particularly good at recognizing patterns. They consist of layers of interconnected nodes or "neurons", and each connection has a weight that is adjusted as the network learns. Neural networks are what power deep learning, a subfield of machine learning that's behind many of the most exciting advancements in AI, including self-driving cars and voice assistants like Siri and Alexa.

In the sandwich-making example, if we were to train an AI to make a sandwich, we would show it many examples of sandwich-making, and it would learn the necessary steps and their order. We could even give it some examples of bad sandwiches, so it learns what not to do!

However, AI learning is not just about recognizing patterns and making decisions based on those patterns. It's also about refining its knowledge and improving its performance over time. This is where reinforcement learning comes in. In reinforcement learning, an AI learns to make decisions by interacting with its environment and receiving feedback, like rewards or punishments. The AI learns to make better decisions over time by maximizing its rewards and minimizing its punishments.

In conclusion, the way AI learns is very much like how we humans learn - by observing, doing, and learning from feedback. It's a fascinating process that's changing the way we live and work.

Machine learning is a method of data analysis, and as such, it heavily relies on data. The data used in machine learning is often categorized as either structured or unstructured.

Structured data is data that is organized in a predefined manner or has a specific form. This includes data in relational databases (tables with rows and columns), spreadsheets, or any other data with a clear, consistent structure. Examples include a list of names, ages, or addresses of a group of people. In machine learning, structured data is often easier to work with because algorithms can easily understand and process this data.

Structured data is often used in machine learning tasks like regression and classification, where each data point (row in a table) has several attributes or features (columns in the table). For example, if we were trying to predict house prices (a typical machine learning task), structured data could include attributes like the number of bedrooms, the size of the house, the location, and so on. Each of these features can be quantified or categorized in a structured way.

Unstructured data, on the other hand, doesn't follow a predefined data model or isn't organized in a predefined manner. It could be textual data, images, audio, video, social media posts, and so on. Machine learning can still process and analyze unstructured data, but it usually requires additional preprocessing to structure the data in a way that the algorithm can understand.

For instance, if we were building a machine learning model to analyze customer reviews (which is text data -

an example of unstructured data), we might need to perform steps like text tokenization (breaking text down into individual words), removal of irrelevant words, and conversion of words into numerical vectors (a process called word embedding) before a machine learning algorithm could use the data for training.

In both cases, understanding your data - whether it's structured or unstructured - is crucial. You need to know what kind of data you have, what it represents, and how to process it effectively to get good results from your machine learning model.

Remember that structured data is like a neatly arranged bookshelf where each book (data point) has a specific place based on its characteristics. On the other hand, unstructured data is more like a pile of books where you need to make an effort to sort and understand the books based on their content. Both types of data have their place in machine learning, and understanding them is a crucial part of the process.

The Role of Mathematics in AI

Mathematics is like a backstage magician working tirelessly to ensure AI performs as expected. It's the foundation of all AI systems, even though it may not be visible on the surface. Let's break down how mathematics plays a part in AI, and why it's so important.

1.   Understanding and interpreting data: AI systems work with huge amounts of data, and mathematics helps us make sense of that data. Concepts like mean, median, mode, and standard deviation are used to understand data trends and variability. Probability and statistics are used to make predictions and analyze the likelihood of certain outcomes.

2.   Building models: Machine learning, a subset of AI, uses mathematical models to make predictions or decisions without being explicitly programmed to perform the task. These models are essentially mathematical equations that take in data and output predictions. For example, linear regression, a basic machine learning technique, uses a simple equation ($y = ax + b$) to predict a response (y) based on the input variable (x).

3. Optimization: Once we have a model, we want it to be the best it can be. This is where optimization comes in. The process of training a machine learning model involves adjusting its parameters to minimize the difference between its predictions and actual values, a process called minimizing the loss function. This is essentially a mathematical optimization problem.

4. Geometry and Algebra: Concepts from geometry and algebra are used extensively in AI. For example, vectors and matrices (from linear algebra) are used to represent and manipulate data. Distance measures, like Euclidean distance, are used to quantify the similarity between different data points.

5. Logic and Algorithms: Logical reasoning is at the heart of many AI systems, especially those that need to make decisions based on a set of rules or constraints. Also, algorithms, which are step-by-step mathematical procedures, are used to design and implement AI systems.

So, while you might not see mathematical equations when you're chatting with an AI or getting recommendations from it, remember that there's a whole world of mathematics working behind the scenes!

Introduction to Generative AI

When we talk about artificial intelligence (AI), we often refer to systems or models that can understand, learn, and act based on the data fed to them. But what if we took it a step further? What if these AI models could not just understand and learn, but also create? This is where Generative AI comes into play.

Generative AI is a type of artificial intelligence that focuses on generating something new. It's like an artist of the AI world, capable of creating new content that's never existed before. This could be anything from writing a poem, composing music, creating art, designing new fashion styles, to even generating entirely new ideas or concepts. It's a fascinating branch of AI that really pushes the boundaries of what machines can do.

What is Generative AI?

Generative AI models are, at their core, systems that can generate new, unique outputs based on the patterns they've learned from their training data. These models don't just mimic the input data but can generate completely new instances that resemble the input data.

Let's take an example to illustrate this. Imagine you have a generative AI model that's been trained on a dataset of classical music. After its training, you ask it to generate a new piece of music. The AI won't just copy a piece of music from its training data. Instead, it will create an entirely new piece of music that sounds like it belongs in the classical genre, based on what it's learned about the patterns and structure of classical music.

This ability to generate new content is what sets generative AI apart from other types of AI. It's not just about understanding the data or making predictions based on it. It's about creating something new and unique that still fits within the parameters of what it's learned.

Generative AI is a powerful tool and its potential applications are vast. It can be used to generate realistic images for video games or virtual reality, write songs, design new molecules for drug discovery, generate realistic speech for voice assistants, and much more. However, as with any technology, it's important to use it responsibly and be aware of the ethical implications of its use.

Understanding Generative AI requires some knowledge of more complex concepts like neural networks and specific types of generative models like Generative Adversarial Networks (GANs) and others. We'll dive deeper into these topics in the upcoming sections, exploring how these models mimic the human brain, how they generate new content, and how they're applied in fields like natural language processing. Stay tuned!

Basics of Neural Networks and How They Mimic the Human Brain

Imagine the human brain. It's a mind-bogglingly complex organ, filled with billions of neurons that interact to create our thoughts, experiences, and behaviors. Now, what if we could design a computer system that mimics this structure and function? Enter: Neural Networks.

Neural Networks are a category of algorithms in machine learning designed to model the way neurons in our brain interact and process information. Each neuron in a neural network takes in some input, processes it, and passes it on - much like the neurons in our brain. Let's simplify it a bit more.

Neurons: The Building Blocks

Just like a building is made of individual bricks, a neural network is made of individual nodes or "neurons". Each neuron takes multiple inputs, applies some calculation to them, and produces an output. Think of it as a mini decision-maker.

In our brains, a neuron might receive inputs in the form of sensory information, decide what to do based on that information, and then send signals to other neurons.

Similarly, in a neural network, a neuron receives data, performs a calculation, and then sends the result to other neurons.

Layers: From Input to Output

Neural networks are organized into layers. There's an input layer that receives the raw data, one or more "hidden" layers that process this data, and an output layer that delivers the final result.

Just like how our sensory organs first pick up information (input layer), our brain processes it (hidden layers), and then we react (output layer), a neural network functions in a similar flow.

Learning: Getting Smarter

Here's where things get really interesting. Neural networks, much like us, can learn from experience. They do this through a process called "training". During training, the network is exposed to lots of data and makes predictions based on that data.

When the network makes a mistake (i.e., its

prediction doesn't match the known answer), it goes back and adjusts the calculations inside its neurons. This is similar to how we humans learn from our mistakes and change our behavior accordingly. This iterative process of guessing, checking the answer, and then adjusting continues until the network gets better at making correct predictions.

Weights and Biases: Fine-tuning the Decisions

The 'adjustments' we talked about are actually changes to specific parameters within the neurons, known as 'weights' and 'biases'. These determine how much importance a neuron gives to its inputs. For example, when deciding whether or not to carry an umbrella, your brain might give more weight to the dark clouds in the sky (input) than the fact that it's a summer month.

In a similar way, by adjusting weights and biases during training, a neural network learns which inputs are important and which aren't for making accurate predictions.

So, in essence, neural networks are computer algorithms that mimic the structure and learning process of our brain, taking in data, learning from it, and making decisions or predictions. They form the basis of many advanced AI systems and are a core part of generative AI models, which we'll explore further in the upcoming sections.

Weights and Biases: Fine-tuning the Decisions

- This is a concept that has caught the attention of many due to its unique approach and fascinating capabilities. This concept is called Generative Adversarial Networks, or GANs for short.

- Let's imagine you're an art enthusiast who has just learned to paint. You create a painting and show it to your teacher, who then critiques it and gives you suggestions on how to improve. You take these suggestions into account, make the necessary adjustments, and create a new painting. This process is repeated until your teacher can't distinguish your art from that of a professional artist. This, in a nutshell, is how GANs work.

- GANs are a type of artificial intelligence model used in unsupervised machine learning. They were introduced by Ian Goodfellow and his colleagues in 2014. GANs consist of two main components: a Generator and a Discriminator, which work together in a sort of competition.

The Generator's job is to create new data that

resembles the real data. Think of it as an artist creating a painting. The Generator starts with some random noise (a bunch of random numbers), and its goal is to transform this noise into something that resembles the real data.

- The Discriminator, on the other hand, is like the art teacher. It takes in both real data and the data created by the Generator, and its job is to distinguish between the two. It critiques the Generator's work, telling it how well it did in creating data that resembles the real thing.

- The Generator and Discriminator are both neural networks, and they learn together in a game. The Generator tries to make data that will fool the Discriminator, and the Discriminator tries to get better at distinguishing real data from fake data. Over time, the Generator gets better and better at creating realistic data, until the Discriminator can't tell the difference. At this point, the Generator is producing very realistic data!

One of the most exciting applications of GANs is in the creation of new, realistic images. For example, GANs have been used to create images of people who do not exist but look incredibly real. They've also been used in art, fashion, and even video games.

- It's important to note, however, that while GANs are powerful, they are also complex and can be challenging to train. Since the Generator and Discriminator are essentially playing a game, if one of them becomes too powerful too quickly, it can dominate the other, leading to poor results. This is known as 'mode collapse,' and it's one of the many challenges researchers face when working with GANs.

- In conclusion, GANs are a fascinating and powerful type of machine learning model. They use a competitive process between two neural networks to generate new, realistic data, leading to a wide range of exciting applications. Despite their complexities and challenges, GANs continue to be a hot topic in the field of AI due to their potential.

What is Natural Language Processing?

Imagine you're chatting with your friend over a messaging app. You type in words, sentences, emojis, and your friend understands what you're saying. Now, what if you could chat in the same way with a computer and it could understand and respond just like your friend? That's the magic of Natural Language Processing (NLP)!

NLP is a branch of artificial intelligence (AI) that helps computers understand, interpret, and generate human language. This means it's all about how computers can be programmed to understand our natural, human language.

If you've ever asked Siri a question, or had a chat with a customer support bot, you've seen NLP in action. It's what allows these systems to understand and respond to your questions in a human-like way. Without NLP, computers would struggle to understand our language because it's full of nuances, idioms, and structures that we, as humans, easily understand but are difficult for a machine.

How does NLP work?

- Text Processing: First, the raw text data needs to be cleaned and organized. This involves removing unnecessary elements like punctuation, special characters, and numbers. It also includes "tokenization", where the text is broken down into individual words or "tokens".

- Parts of Speech Tagging: The next step is understanding the role of each word in a sentence. Is it a noun, a verb, an adjective, etc? This helps the computer understand the sentence structure.

- Named Entity Recognition: This is all about identifying the important elements in a text. For example, in the sentence "OpenAI developed GPT-3", OpenAI is an organization, and GPT-3 is a product.

- Sentiment Analysis: This is about understanding the emotion behind the text. Is the sentiment positive, negative, or neutral? This is commonly used in social media monitoring, product reviews, etc.

- Topic Modeling: This is about finding the main themes in a large amount of text. For example, if you have thousands of articles, topic modeling can help group them into topics.

Applications of NLP

NLP is used in many areas of technology and business, including:

- Search Engines: Google uses NLP to understand your search queries and provide relevant results.
- Voice Assistants: Siri, Alexa, and Google Assistant use NLP to understand and respond to voice commands.
- Machine Translation: Services like Google Translate use NLP to translate text or speech from one language to another.
- Social Media Monitoring: Companies use NLP to analyze social media posts for sentiment about their brand.

So, in short, NLP is about creating a bridge between machines and humans, enabling them to have a conversation. It's a complex and exciting field that's at the heart of many of the technologies we use every day!

In the world of machine learning, there are many types of models that can generate new data that resembles the data they were trained on. These models are called "generative models". Let's talk about a few popular ones:

- Autoencoders (AE): Think of Autoencoders as artists who can both create and critique their own work. They are composed of two parts: an encoder that learns to compress data, and a decoder that learns to reconstruct the original data from the compressed version. Autoencoders can be used to reduce noise in images, fill in missing data, or generate new data that resembles the training data.

- Variational Autoencoders (VAE): VAEs are a type of autoencoder with a twist. Instead of directly learning to compress data, they learn to represent data as a distribution (like a bell curve or a scatter plot). This allows them to generate new data that is similar but not identical to the training data, leading to more diversity in the output.

- Generative Adversarial Networks (GAN): GANs are like a team of a forger and a detective. The forger (generator) tries to create fake data, and the detective (discriminator) tries to tell if the data is real or fake. The forger learns from the detective's feedback and gets better over time. GANs have been used to generate impressively realistic images, music, and even text.

- Transformer-based models (like GPT): These models are based on the Transformer architecture, which was initially designed for tasks like translating languages. However, with some modifications (like training it to predict the next word in a sentence), it can be used as a generative model. GPT (Generative Pretrained Transformer), which you're interacting with right now, is an example of this!
- PixelCNN: This is a type of model that generates images pixel by pixel, starting from the top-left corner and moving across the image one pixel at a time. It uses a clever trick to ensure that each pixel it generates is only influenced by the pixels that came before it.

Each of these models has its own strengths and weaknesses, and the best model to use depends on the specific task at hand. Some are better for images, some for text, and some for other types of data. But all of them are examples of the amazing things that can be done with generative models in machine learning!

Exploring Multiple models and how they work!

Understanding Chatbots and Conversational AI

- Chatbots are like helpful robots that live on your computer or phone. They are programs designed to chat with you, just like a human would, except they're not human, they're software. Think of them like your own personal assistant, ready to answer questions or help you with tasks at any time of the day.

- Chatbots can live in many different places: they can be on a website, in an app on your phone, on social media platforms like Facebook, or even in your email. They are there to help you with a wide range of tasks. For instance, a chatbot on a shopping website might help you find the right product, while a chatbot in a banking app might help you check your account balance.

- Now, let's talk about "Conversational AI." This might sound like a fancy term, but it's really just a way of saying that these chatbots are designed to have conversations that feel natural and human-like.

- The goal of Conversational AI is to make it seem like you're chatting with another person, not a machine. This is done by using techniques from a field of study called Natural Language Processing, or NLP. NLP is all about helping computers understand, respond to, and learn from human language in a meaningful way.
- Chatbots powered by Conversational AI can do things like understand what you're saying (or typing), figure out what you need, and then respond in a way that makes sense. They can even learn from their interactions with people to improve their responses over time.
- So in short, Chatbots and Conversational AI are all about creating software that can chat with us in a way that feels natural and human-like, making it easier for us to interact with our devices and get the help we need.
- Next, we'll move on to discussing more about how these chatbots work and how they are trained. But for now, just remember: chatbots are like your personal, automated helpers, and Conversational AI is what makes those helpers able to understand and respond to you in a natural way.

ChatGPT: A Chatbot by OpenAI

ChatGPT, a prominent example of a chatbot, is developed by OpenAI. The 'GPT' in ChatGPT stands for 'Generative Pre-training Transformer', which might sound a bit technical, but don't worry! Let's break it down in simple terms.

Generative simply means that this chatbot can create or 'generate' responses or content on its own. When you ask ChatGPT a question, it doesn't look up pre-written answers; instead, it creates an answer right on the spot, just for you!

Pre-training refers to the initial training phase of the model. Before ChatGPT talks to anyone, it learns about language and the world by reading a vast amount of text from the internet. It's similar to how a human child learns by observing and absorbing information from their surroundings.

Transformer is the type of AI model that ChatGPT is based on. Without getting into the complex math, think of transformers as a type of model that's really good at understanding context in language. They help ChatGPT understand not just individual words, but whole sentences and even longer pieces of text.

Now that we understand the name, let's look at how ChatGPT works and how it's trained.

How ChatGPT Works and How It's Trained

- Pre-training: Remember when we said that ChatGPT learns from reading a lot of internet text? This is where that happens. During pre-training, ChatGPT is exposed to a diverse range of internet text. However, it doesn't know specifics about which documents were in its training set or have access to any specific documents or sources. It's important to understand that this phase is about learning patterns in the data, not memorizing it.

- Fine-tuning: After pre-training, the model is further trained on a narrower dataset, generated with the help of human reviewers who follow specific guidelines provided by OpenAI. This process fine-tunes the model's behavior, making it more controlled, safe, and useful.

As you interact with ChatGPT, it predicts what to say next based on the conversation history. When you send a message to ChatGPT, it adds your message to the list of inputs and generates a response. It does this by estimating the probability of each possible next word, choosing the most likely word, and repeating this process until it reaches the end of its response.

While this is a simplified explanation, it covers the essence of how ChatGPT works. It's a machine learning model that learns patterns of human language during its pre-training phase and then gets fine-tuned to be safe and useful. As you chat with it, it generates responses based on what it predicts you're expecting as the next part of the conversation.

Understanding the concept of chatbots and how they work can be a lot to take in, especially for beginners. But, as we've seen with ChatGPT, they're essentially software applications trained to communicate with humans in a natural, conversational manner. Whether it's for customer service, entertainment, or education, chatbots like ChatGPT are a fascinating example of the practical application of AI in our everyday.

(CHATGPT HAS TURNED OUT TO BE ONE OF THE GREATEST BREAKTHROUGHS IN THE WORLD OF AI, AND IT HAS GREAT POTENTIAL. I HAVE WRITTEN AN ENTIRE BOOK ON HOW TO USE CHATGPT TO EARN GOOD MONEY. MORE ON THIS CAN BE FOUND IN THE AUTHOR'S NOTE AT THE END OF THE BOOK)

Exploring Bard by Google

Bard by Google is a chatbot developed by Google AI. It uses a vast dataset of text and code to generate responses that resemble human-like text, covering a wide range of prompts and questions. For instance, Bard can offer factual topic summaries, craft creative content, and provide assistance with homework.

Bard is trained through Reinforcement Learning from Human Feedback (RLHF), which involves soliciting ratings from a large group of human judges regarding the quality of Bard's generated text. Based on these ratings, Bard receives rewards for producing text that garners high evaluations.

The RLHF training method presents several benefits over traditional language model training approaches. Firstly, it enables Bard to learn from real-world feedback rather than relying solely on a predefined dataset of text. Consequently, Bard can generate contextually relevant text that is responsive to ongoing conversations, rather than merely reproducing information from a fixed dataset. Secondly,

RLHF facilitates Bard in acquiring the ability to generate text in various styles. For instance, it can learn to generate formal text suitable for business emails or informal text suited for casual conversations.

Lastly, RLHF is considered by many as a more efficient means of training a language model compared to traditional methods. This efficiency arises from Bard only needing to be trained on a limited number of examples, instead of an extensive dataset of text.

While still under development, Bard has already acquired proficiency in numerous tasks, including summarizing factual topics, producing creative content such as poems, stories, and scripts, assisting users with their homework, and answering questions comprehensively and informatively.

Bard is a versatile tool that holds potential to revolutionize human-computer interactions. Its impact can extend to various domains such as education, business, and entertainment

Introduction to Midjourney

Midjourney is an artificial intelligence program that generates images based on written descriptions, also known as "prompts." It was created by a company based in San Francisco, California, led by David Holz, who was also a co-founder of Leap Motion. Midjourney is a powerful tool for creating realistic images from text descriptions. It works by learning from a large dataset of real-world images, training a neural network to understand the relationship between text and images. Once trained, it can generate unique and high-quality images based on given prompts.

To use Midjourney, you can interact with a bot on the Discord platform. Simply use the /imagine command followed by your description or prompt, and the bot will return a set of four images based on your input. This makes it easy for artists and other creative professionals to quickly visualize their ideas and concepts.

The company behind Midjourney has been continuously improving the platform, releasing new versions every few months. Each version aims to enhance the model's understanding of prompts and improve image generation. Artists have found Midjourney useful for creating rough drafts of their artistic concepts to show clients before starting the actual work. It allows them to quickly visualize ideas without spending a lot of time on initial sketches. However, concerns have been raised about the potential devaluation of original creative work if artists' art is used to train the AI. To address this, Midjourney has a policy that allows artists to request the removal of their work if they believe their copyright has been violated.

The advertising industry has also embraced AI tools like Midjourney. It offers opportunities for creating original content, brainstorming ideas quickly, and making e-commerce advertising more efficient. With Midjourney, custom ads for individuals and special effects can be easily created.

Midjourney is a closed-source model that requires a monthly subscription fee for access. It is known for producing high-quality images that are often indistinguishable from real photographs. If you're interested in creating realistic and unique images from text descriptions, Midjourney is definitely worth considering.

STABLE DIFFUSION

Stable Diffusion is another text-to-image AI model that generates realistic images from text descriptions. Developed by Stability AI, it specializes in AI for creative applications. Like Midjourney, it learns to generate images from a large dataset of real-world images, training a neural network to understand the relationship between text descriptions and images.

To create an image, Stable Diffusion starts with a random image and uses the neural network to refine it iteratively until it matches the text description. This process continues until the image is considered satisfactory. Stable Diffusion has already produced impressive images of people, animals, objects, as well as fictional characters and scenes.

While Stable Diffusion is still under development, it has the potential to revolutionize art creation and consumption. It's a powerful tool for generating realistic images from text prompts.

Additionally, there's a difference in accessibility. Midjourney is primarily accessed through a Discord bot, while Stable Diffusion is available for free online and can be used on any computer with a GPU.

Both Midjourney and Stable Diffusion are valuable tools in the field of text-to-image generation. They offer exciting possibilities for creating realistic and unique images based on textual descriptions.

RUNWAY AI

Runway AI is an artificial intelligence (AI) company that develops tools for creatives. Their flagship product is Runway Studio, a cloud-based platform that allows users to create videos, images, and text with the help of AI.

Runway Studio uses a variety of AI techniques, including natural language processing (NLP), computer vision (CV), and machine learning (ML), to generate creative content. For example, Runway Studio can be used to generate text descriptions of images, create videos from text prompts, or edit videos using natural language commands.

Runway AI was founded in 2020 by a team of artists and engineers who believe that AI can be used to empower creatives. The company is headquartered in San Francisco, California.

Here are some of the things that Runway AI can do:

- Generate text descriptions of images: Runway AI can be used to generate text descriptions of images. This can be useful for tasks such as creating image captions, generating marketing copy, or writing product descriptions.

- Create videos from text prompts: Runway AI can be used to create videos from text prompts. This can be useful for tasks such as creating explainer videos, generating marketing videos, or creating personal videos.

- Edit videos using natural language commands: Runway AI can be used to edit videos using natural language commands. This can be useful for tasks such as trimming videos, adding text to videos, or changing the speed of videos.

Runway AI is still under development, but it has the potential to revolutionize the way that creatives work. By making AI tools more accessible and easier to use, Runway AI is helping to empower creatives to create new and innovative content.

TEXT-TO-AUDIO

Text-to-audio AI is a type of artificial intelligence that can convert text into spoken audio. This technology has been around for many years, but it has only recently become commercially viable due to the development of deep learning algorithms. Deep learning algorithms are a type of machine learning algorithm that can learn from large amounts of data. In the case of text-to-audio AI, deep learning algorithms are trained on large datasets of audio recordings of human speech. This allows the algorithms to learn the nuances of human speech, such as the correct pronunciation of words, the correct intonation of sentences, and the correct pacing of speech.

As a result of the development of deep learning algorithms, text-to-audio AI has become much more realistic in recent years. In the past, text-to-audio AI voices often sounded robotic and unnatural. However, with the development of deep learning algorithms, text-to-audio AI voices can now sound very realistic. In fact, some text-to-audio AI voices are so realistic that it is difficult to tell them apart from human speech.

There are a number of commercial applications for text-to-audio AI. For example, text-to-audio AI can be used to create audiobooks, podcasts, and other types of audio content. Text-to-audio AI can also be used to create educational materials, such as lectures and tutorials. Additionally, text-to-audio AI can be used to create marketing materials, such as product demonstrations and commercials.

As text-to-audio AI technology continues to develop, it is likely that we will see even more commercial applications for this technology. For example, text-to-audio AI could be used to create personalized audiobooks that are tailored to the individual listener's interests. Additionally, text-to-audio AI could be used to create virtual assistants that can provide information and assistance to users in a natural and engaging way.

Here are some examples of how text-to-audio AI is being used commercially today:

- Amazon Polly: Amazon Polly is a cloud-based service that can be used to create realistic human-like voices from text. Amazon Polly is used by a variety of businesses, including Audible, Pearson, and Samsung.

- Google Cloud Text-to-Speech: Google Cloud Text-to-Speech is a cloud-based service that can be used to create realistic human-like voices from text. Google Cloud Text-to-Speech is used by a variety of businesses, including Spotify, Netflix, and Disney.

- IBM Watson Speech to Text: IBM Watson Speech to Text is a cloud-based service that can be used to convert speech into text. IBM Watson Speech to Text is used by a variety of businesses, including Comcast, Cisco, and Wells Fargo.

How Generative AI Model Works

To understand generative AI models, think about sculptors. Sculptors take a block of marble and, using their tools and skill, shape it into something new. A generative AI model operates similarly, but instead of marble, it works with data. It's trained to take a large set of data and generate new data that's similar but not identical to the original. This could be anything from a piece of text, a picture, a piece of music, or even a 3D model.

Basic structure of these models and the concept of 'transformers'

A generative AI model is built upon various architectural designs, with one of the most popular being 'transformers'. Transformers are named so because of their ability to transform input data (like a sentence) into output data (like a translated sentence or a response) while understanding the structure and context of the input.

Think of transformers as master linguists. They don't

just translate words one by one. Instead, they understand the entire sentence structure and then recreate it in another language, ensuring the translated sentence makes sense. This is because transformers, unlike previous models, can consider all words or data points at once rather than just looking at them in isolation.

Understanding attention mechanisms: How AI focuses

In the realm of AI, attention mechanisms play a crucial role. They allow the model to focus on certain parts of the data while ignoring others. Think of it like when you're reading a book - you focus on the storyline and important details while glossing over less crucial information.

In the same way, an attention mechanism allows AI to focus on important parts of the data. For instance, when generating a sentence about cats, words and concepts related to cats will be given more "attention," allowing the AI to generate more relevant and coherent sentences.

The process of training and fine-tuning AI models

Training an AI model is quite similar to teaching a child. It starts with simple tasks and gradually moves to more complex ones. The AI model learns from a large set of example data during training. It then generates its own data and compares it with the correct output. If there's a mistake, the model adjusts its internal parameters to minimize the error. This process is repeated with multiple examples until the model gets better at generating the correct output.

Fine-tuning is a process that comes after the initial training. This involves further training the model on a smaller, more specific dataset. Think of it as specializing in a particular field after general education. For instance, a model trained on general English text can be fine-tuned to generate medical articles by training it further on medical texts.

Limitations, challenges, and ethical considerations in AI

Like all technologies, AI has its limitations. It can only generate data based on what it has seen during training. It doesn't have the capability to understand or create something totally new.

Moreover, there are challenges associated with ensuring that the AI model behaves as expected. AI models can sometimes generate incorrect, nonsensical, or even harmful outputs if not monitored carefully. This leads us to ethical considerations. It's crucial to ensure that the AI models are trained and used responsibly, without causing harm to individuals or society.

In conclusion, generative AI models are powerful tools that can create new data from what they've learned. They use concepts like transformers and attention mechanisms to understand and generate data, and their effectiveness improves through the processes of training and fine-tuning. However, like any tool, they must be used wisely and responsibly, considering their limitations and ethical implications.

AI IN HEALTHCARE

Artificial intelligence (AI) is rapidly transforming the healthcare industry. AI-powered technologies are being used to improve patient care, reduce costs, and improve efficiency.

Here's a breakdown of how AI is impacting healthcare:

- Detecting Diseases: AI is advancing the way doctors diagnose diseases, including conditions like kidney disease. It can analyze medical images and data, highlighting important details that might be overlooked.
- Organizing Health Information: The healthcare industry deals with huge amounts of complex data, ranging from X-rays and doctor's notes to genetic information. AI is playing a significant role in structuring this data, making it more accessible and usable.
- Predicting Health Outcomes: AI has the ability to analyze a patient's health data and predict potential outcomes, such as the likelihood of hospitalization or a COVID-19 diagnosis. This predictive capability allows for more proactive and personalized patient care.
- Accelerating Research: AI is being used in research

- studies to quickly analyze large amounts of health data. For instance, AI was used in a cancer center to rapidly find suitable patients for their studies, speeding up the research process significantly.

Moreover, AI is expanding its reach in healthcare:

- Medical Imaging: AI is being used to analyze medical images, such as X-rays and MRIs, to detect diseases and abnormalities earlier and more accurately.
- Drug Discovery: AI has the capability to analyze large datasets of genetic and medical data, helping in the discovery of new drugs and treatments for diseases.
- Personalized Medicine: By analyzing a patient's medical history, genetic data, and lifestyle factors, AI can help create personalized treatment plans, improving the effectiveness of care.
- Telemedicine: AI is enhancing telemedicine services, such as virtual consultations and remote health monitoring, making healthcare more accessible to patients regardless of their location.

AI is a vital tool in healthcare today. It is enhancing accuracy in diagnoses, making data handling efficient, predicting health outcomes, and speeding up research. AI is truly reshaping healthcare, with more advancements expected in the future.

Understanding Deepfakes

Deepfakes are like digital masks. Picture this: You're watching a video of your favorite celebrity doing something outrageous. But there's a catch — that's not really the celebrity. It's their face, their voice, but the actions are controlled by someone else entirely. This is what deepfakes can do. They allow someone to take the face and voice of another person and use them in a video that the original person never acted in or even knew about.

Deepfakes are the result of AI techniques that have learned to create highly convincing counterfeit content. The name "deepfake" is derived from "deep learning", a type of AI method, and "fake", signaling the artificial nature of the content.

Introduction to deepfakes and their connection to Generative AI

To understand how deepfakes work, let's recall our discussion on generative AI. As we've previously discussed, generative AI models are like artists that use data as their raw material to create new, unique pieces. In the case of deepfakes, the generative AI is creating videos.

Deepfakes are created using a type of generative AI model known as a Generative Adversarial Network, or GAN. If you remember, a GAN consists of two parts — a Generator and a Discriminator. The Generator creates fake videos, and the Discriminator tries to tell the difference between real videos and the ones created by the Generator.

It's a bit like a game of digital cops and robbers. The Generator (the robber) tries to make a fake video that's so good the Discriminator (the cop) can't tell it's fake. If the Discriminator catches the fake, the Generator learns from its mistake and tries again. This game continues until the Generator becomes so good at creating fakes that the Discriminator can't tell the difference.

The result is a deepfake — a video that looks and sounds like a real person but is entirely artificial.

The process of creating a deepfake requires a large amount of data. For example, to create a deepfake of a celebrity, the AI needs many pictures and videos of that celebrity. The more data it has, the better the resulting deepfake will be.

But why would anyone want to create a deepfake? There are several reasons, and they're not all bad.

The impact of deepfakes: the good, the bad, and the ugly

On the positive side, deepfakes can be used in film and TV production. For instance, they can be used to revive actors who have passed away, or to make a younger version of an actor. Deepfakes can also be used in education, for example, to bring historical figures to life. However, there are also negative aspects to deepfakes. They can be used to create fake news, spread misinformation, or to defame individuals. They pose a real challenge to information integrity, as it becomes difficult to trust what we see and hear.

Tools and technologies used to create and detect deepfakes

There are numerous tools available to create deepfakes, ranging from open-source software to advanced AI models. Detecting deepfakes is a bit trickier. It requires other AI models that have been trained to spot the subtle signs that a video is a deepfake. This is an ongoing area of research, as the better we get at creating deepfakes, the harder they become to detect.

In conclusion, deepfakes are a fascinating and somewhat alarming development in the field of AI. They showcase the power of generative AI models, but also highlight the ethical and societal challenges these technologies can pose. As with all technology, the key is to use it responsibly and stay informed about its potential

Deepfakes, if misused, can have far-reaching consequences:

1. Spreading misinformation: Deepfakes can be weaponized to fabricate false narratives about individuals or organizations, causing harm to reputations and potentially inciting conflict. For instance, a well-crafted deepfake video could falsely depict a public figure engaging in illegal activities or making inflammatory statements. If disseminated widely, such a video could manipulate public opinion, tarnish the individual's reputation, and even lead to real-world violence.

2. Influencing elections: In the political sphere, deepfakes can be used to manipulate the electoral process. By creating fake videos of politicians making false promises or engaging in misconduct, bad actors can mislead voters and influence election outcomes. Given the viral nature of social media, such deceptive videos can quickly reach a wide audience and sow doubt and confusion.

3. Harassing or bullying people: Deepfakes can also be exploited to harass or bully individuals. For example, a person's face could be swapped onto another's body in a compromising situation, creating embarrassing or damaging content. Such content could be used for revenge, blackmail, or cyberbullying, causing immense psychological harm to the victim.

4. Committing fraud: The financial sector isn't immune to the threat of deepfakes either. By creating convincing deepfake videos or audio, fraudsters can impersonate individuals for monetary gain. For instance, a deepfake video could show a person approving a financial transaction or giving out personal information. This could potentially be used to trick banks, companies, or individuals into transferring money or disclosing sensitive information.

EXAMPLE

1. To help you understand this with an example :

Manipulating public opinion:
In a fictional political campaign, Candidate A is running against Candidate B for a highly contested position. A deepfake video emerges, seemingly showing Candidate A confessing to illegal activities and making derogatory remarks about certain communities. The video quickly goes viral, spreading across social media platforms and news outlets. Despite being entirely fabricated, the deepfake casts doubt on Candidate A's integrity and leads to a decline in public support. This example illustrates how deepfakes can be used to manipulate public opinion, discredit individuals, and impact the outcome of an election.

2 : Personal impersonation and privacy violation:
In a fictional scenario, Emily is a successful entrepreneur who has a substantial social media following. An individual with ill intentions creates a deepfake video that convincingly portrays Emily engaging in illegal or immoral activities. The deepfake video is released online, rapidly gaining traction and reaching Emily's professional network, friends, and family. The impact on Emily's personal and professional life is devastating, as her

reputation is tarnished, relationships are strained, and her business suffers. This is just one example of the harmful consequences that can arise from the use of Deepfakes.

Applications and Future of Generative AI

Generative AI is a subset of artificial intelligence that involves machines creating new content or ideas, often through the use of machine learning algorithms. It's an exciting and rapidly evolving field with numerous applications across different industries.

1. Art and Design: Generative AI has found a place in art and design, where it's being used to create everything from paintings to music to interior designs. For instance, AI algorithms have been trained to generate new pieces of art that resemble the styles of famous painters, or compose music in the style of classical composers.

2. Content Creation: Generative AI is also being used in content creation, such as writing articles or generating realistic images and videos. For example, AI can generate human-like text, enabling the production of large volumes of written content at a faster rate.

3. Scientific Research: In the realm of scientific research, generative AI can be used to generate hypotheses or design experiments. It can also create virtual models of complex systems, such as weather

patterns or biological systems, to study their behavior under different conditions.

4 : Product Development: Companies are using generative AI in product development to generate and test new ideas. This can drastically speed up the innovation process, as AI can generate and evaluate a multitude of design options in a short amount of time.

As we look to the future, we can expect the capabilities and applications of generative AI to continue to expand. With advancements in machine learning techniques, AI systems will be able to generate more complex and creative outputs, from sophisticated video games and virtual reality experiences, to groundbreaking scientific discoveries and innovative products.

Real-world applications of generative AI and deepfakes

While deepfakes are often associated with negative uses such as misinformation and nonconsensual pornography, it's important to note that the underlying technology has numerous beneficial applications as well.

- Entertainment Industry: Deepfakes can be used in movies and TV shows to generate realistic special effects. For instance, they can be used to de-age actors, replicate performances, or even bring deceased actors back to the screen.

- Language Translation: Deepfakes can be utilized for real-time translation in video calls, making conversations between people who speak different languages more seamless. In one impressive example, a video showed soccer star David Beckham speaking fluently in nine languages, achieved through deepfake technology.

- Education and Training: Deepfakes can be used to create realistic scenarios for training purposes. For example, they can be used to generate simulations for medical training, crisis management drills, or virtual reality learning experiences.

The future potential of generative AI and deepfakes is vast. As these technologies continue to advance, they will likely become more integrated into our everyday lives, providing novel solutions to complex problems and offering new ways of creating and interacting with digital content.

Ethical considerations, societal impact, and AI policy

However, as with any powerful technology, the use of generative AI and deepfakes comes with important ethical considerations. While these tools can be used for good, they can also be misused in ways that harm individuals or society.

For instance, deepfakes pose a significant threat in the form of misinformation and deception. They can be used to create convincing but false content that could potentially influence public opinion, incite violence, or damage reputations. Nonconsensual pornography, which currently accounts for 96 percent of deepfakes deployed on the Internet, is another major concern.

To mitigate these risks, it's crucial to develop and enforce policies that regulate the use of AI and deepfake technology. This could involve legislation that penalizes misuse, as well as guidelines for tech companies to follow in developing and deploying these technologies

Case Study 1: AI for Good – Predicting Diabetic Retinopathy

In 2016, Google's AI subsidiary, DeepMind, collaborated with Moorfields Eye Hospital NHS Foundation Trust to develop an AI system that could analyze eye scans for signs of diabetic retinopathy, a condition that can lead to blindness if untreated. Traditional analysis of these scans by human experts is time-consuming and often results in a backlog, delaying diagnoses and treatment.

The AI system used a deep learning algorithm trained on thousands of historical de-identified eye scans. It learned to detect and distinguish between healthy patient scans and those with signs of diabetic retinopathy with a high degree of accuracy, comparable to or better than human experts.

A landmark moment came when the AI system was able to identify a patient who was at risk of losing their vision within a 48-hour window, something that might have been missed or delayed if it had relied solely on standard care procedures. The AI's rapid analysis allowed for timely treatment, effectively saving the patient's sight.

This instance became a beacon of AI's potential in healthcare: a blend of high accuracy, speed, and scalability that can have a profound impact on patient outcomes, transforming the way diseases are diagnosed and managed.

Case Study 2 : AI Gone Awry – The Uber Self-Driving Incident

On the evening of March 18, 2018, an autonomous Uber vehicle struck and killed a pedestrian in Tempe, Arizona. The vehicle, although manned by a safety driver, was in autonomous mode. It was a test unit — one of Uber's fleet of self-driving cars, which were seen as the forefront of a new frontier in transportation.

The immediate fallout was significant. Uber suspended all testing of their autonomous vehicles, and the incident became a flashpoint for the debate around the safety of self-driving technology.

Upon investigation, it was revealed that the AI system had indeed detected the pedestrian but had not classified her as a jaywalker needing immediate attention. The system's design did not include a provision for an emergency braking maneuver, leaving that responsibility to the human safety driver, who did not react in time.

This tragedy underscored the nascent risks associated with AI. While the technology promised to reduce traffic accidents caused by human error, it also introduced new complexities and ethical dilemmas about machine decision-making, especially in critical, life-threatening scenarios.

The incident was a sobering reminder of AI's fallibility and the absolute necessity for stringent testing and regulatory oversight. It sparked a global conversation on the safety protocols for AI and pushed for more rigorous standards in autonomous vehicle development.

CONCLUSION

We live in a world that continues to evolve because of new technologies, especially in the area of Artificial Intelligence (AI). AI has grown at an extremely rapid pace, and it doesn't look like it will slow down any time soon. Its impact, from science fiction to real-life applications, has been huge, and it could affect every part of our lives in ways we can't even imagine right now.

When we look around, we can see that this AI change is happening. AI is in every part of our lives, from personalized recommendations on streaming services to voice-activated home assistants to advanced medical diagnostics. It shapes our experiences, interactions, and choices.

What do we need to know? We are at an important moment given how quickly things are changing. We can either adapt and learn or be stressed and left behind. This book is a testament to the former choice. As with any revolution, resisting change might seem like the easier option, but the way to growth and progress is to accept change, learn from it, and adapt to it.

Let's not forget that every big change in technology, like the Internet or the rise of smartphones, has been met with pushback at first. We can't imagine what life would be like without them now. AI is going through a similar change. As we stand on the edge of this huge change, it's important that we choose interest over fear, change over staying the same, and looking forward over denying what's going on.

As the world around us changes, it's important to remember that we're not just watching, we're taking part. We can choose to use AI to make our lives, societies, and the world a better place. It's not enough to just accept technology without questioning it. We need to understand it, learn from it, and use it to our benefit.

Let's welcome the future with open arms, knowing what we know and wanting to learn more. At the end of the day, the future belongs to the people who plan for it now. The AI change is already happening, and the best way to move forward is to learn, adapt, and grow along with it. Let's not fight AI, but instead use its power to build a world we can all be proud of.

THANK-YOU NOTE

Dear Reader,

Thank you for reading this book! I genuinely hope you enjoyed it and gained valuable knowledge from its pages. Remember, learning is an ongoing process that should never cease.

If you found this book to be impactful and insightful, I would like to wholeheartedly request your support by leaving a review. Your feedback is incredibly valuable to me, as it not only helps me improve as an author but also enables other readers to discover and benefit from this book.

Your review will play a crucial role in shaping my future work and assisting fellow individuals in making an informed decision about whether this book is right for them. Your honest thoughts will provide invaluable guidance.

Once again, thank you for your time and for being a part of this journey. Your support means the world to me.

Think of artificial intelligence as more than just a concept or a tool; it's an exciting journey that expands our thinking, unlocking new paths of innovation and progress.

Made in the USA
Monee, IL
22 October 2024